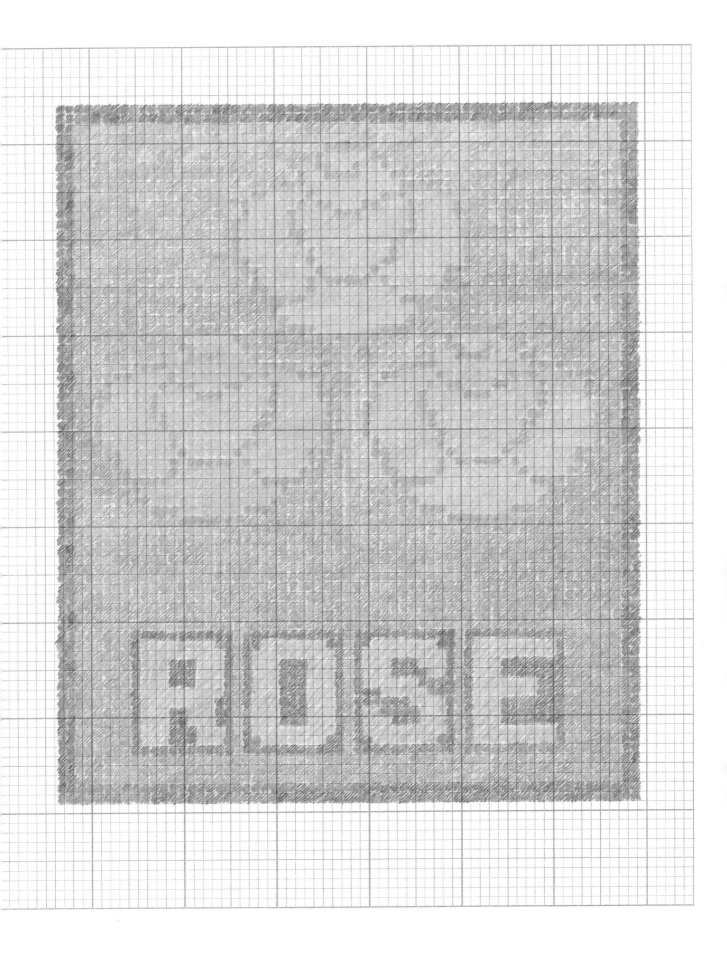

THE PETER RABBIT

CRAFT BOOK

™

DEBBIE SMITH

From the original and authorized stories
BY **BEATRIX POTTER** ™

BLOOMSBURY BOOKS
in association with
FREDERICK WARNE

*These are the finished tapestries made from the charts
on the endpapers of this book (see page 16)*

for ZIGI

BLOOMSBURY BOOKS IN ASSOCIATION WITH FREDERICK WARNE

Published by the Penguin Group
Penguin Books Ltd, 27 Wrights Lane, London W8 5TZ, England
Penguin Books USA Inc., 375 Hudson Street, New York, N.Y. 10014, USA
Penguin Books Australia Ltd, Ringwood, Victoria, Australia
Penguin Books Canada Ltd, 10 Alcorn Avenue, Toronto, Ontario, Canada M4V 3B2
Penguin Books (N.Z.) Ltd, 182-190 Wairau Road, Auckland 10, New Zealand

Penguin Books Ltd, Registered Offices: Harmondsworth, Middlesex, England

Bloomsbury Books, an imprint of Godfrey Cave Group, 42 Bloomsbury Street, London WC1B 3QJ

First published by Frederick Warne & Co. 1987
This edition published 1993
1 3 5 7 9 10 8 6 4 2

Text copyright © Debbie Smith, 1987
Photographs by Chris Lord copyright © Frederick Warne & Co., 1987
Universal Copyright Notice:
Beatrix Potter's original illustrations copyright © Frederick Warne & Co.,
1902, 1903, 1904, 1905, 1906, 1907, 1908, 1909, 1910, 1911, 1918
Copyright in all countries signatory to the Berne Convention
New reproductions copyright © Frederick Warne & Co., 1987
Copyright in all countries signatory to the Berne and Universal Conventions

ISBN 1 85471 310 8

Printed and bound in Great Britain by
William Clowes Limited, Beccles and London

Contents

Introduction

Beatrix Potter wrote the tales about naughty Peter Rabbit and his friends many years ago. In those days, people spent far more time using their hands for both work and leisure than we do now. Traditional craft skills were handed down from parent to child and the entire family would spend many satisfying and pleasurable hours making all sorts of things.

All the projects in this book are based on Beatrix Potter's stories. There isn't enough space to give detailed explanations of every technique used, but if you'd like more information on a particular craft, you could take out a book about it from the library. Don't despair if your finished items are not exactly like the ones in the pictures – it always takes time and practice to perfect making things by hand. Use the book as a source of ideas and no doubt you will soon be designing your own projects anyway.

When you're doing anything messy, please use plenty of newspaper to protect your table and wear an apron (and gloves if necessary) to protect yourself. Needless to say, you won't be in anyone's favour if you don't clear up as soon as you've finished too! You'll need sharp scissors to cut fabric and card neatly so mind the points. Ask an adult to help you with anything tricky such as ironing.

It's always best to read right through the instructions of a project before you start. And most important of all – have fun!

Personalized Handkerchiefs

Ginger and Pickles sold red spotty handkerchiefs at a penny three farthings in their village shop. Perhaps that is where Mrs. Rabbit bought the handkerchief that her naughty son Peter was wrapped in, when he set off with Benjamin Bunny to get back his clothes from Mr. McGregor's garden. You can make a personalized handkerchief with your name on, or somebody else's to give as a present, using any design you like. The handkerchief doesn't have to be a new one, but do remember to wash it first!

To make a personalized handkerchief, you will need:
a clean white (or plain-coloured) handkerchief
a piece of paper to draw your design
stencils (if you want to use them)
clear sticky tape
old sheets of newspaper
soft pencil or dressmaker's (chalk) pencil
paint-on fabric dye

1 Wash, dry and iron the handkerchief, *even if it is new*. (You might want an adult to help you with this.)

2 Measure the handkerchief and draw a square of exactly the same size on a piece of paper, remembering to mark on the handkerchief border if there is one. Work out a design starting with your name, nickname or initials. You can either use stencils for this or draw freehand. Add spots, stripes, flowers or other decorations if you like.

3 Tape the handkerchief on to several thicknesses of newspaper. Copy your design on to it lightly with the dressmaker's (chalk) pencil or soft lead pencil, then paint in the design with the fabric paint.

4 Leave to dry completely, then iron.

Mrs. Tiggy-winkle Pincushion

L ucie discovered Mrs. Tiggy-winkle's home inside the hill when she went in search of her missing handkerchiefs and pinafore dress. Mrs. Tiggy-winkle was a washerwoman, but Lucie also found out that underneath her large apron and striped petticoat, Mrs. Tiggy-winkle was covered in prickles and was, in fact – a *hedgehog*.

To make a Mrs. Tiggy-winkle pincushion you will need:
tracing paper
scissors for paper and fabric
dressmaker's (chalk) pencil (if you have one)
pins
needle and thread
brown felt (approx 20 cm or 8″ square)
cotton wool or kapok for stuffing
3 small beads for eyes and nose
flowery fabric scraps for dress
white fabric scraps for apron and cap
13 mm bias binding tape and lace to trim

1 Trace the pattern pieces and cut them out.

2 Use a dressmaker's (chalk) pencil to draw round pieces A (twice) and B (4 times) on the felt. If you do not have a dressmaker's pencil, just pin the paper pieces on to the felt and cut round them.

3 Sew the bead eyes on to one body piece, as shown on the pattern. Sandwich the 4 feet (B) in position between the 2 body pieces (A) and pin to hold, then sew around the edge of the body (securing the feet) in small running stitches, leaving one side open for stuffing.

4 Stuff firmly (Mrs. Tiggy-winkle is short, but stout) then sew up the opening.

5 To turn up the snout, sew along each snout side again, and pull the cotton to gather tightly. Sew bead nose in position.

6 Cut out dress piece C twice. With right sides together, sew the side and shoulder seams along the dotted lines, then turn right side out. Sew bias binding tape folded in half lengthwise around the neck and armholes. Attach some lace around the neck and hem again with running stitches, making little pleats in it as you go.

7 Cut an oblong 5 × 11 cm (2″ × 4″), a strip 3 × 50 cm (1½″ × 20″) and a circle 8 cm (3″) across in white fabric for the apron and cap.

8 Hem one long and 2 short sides of the oblong, then baste 4 small pleats in the unhemmed edge. Fold in the short ends of the strip, then fold in half lengthwise and fold in the 2 long raw edges (a). Pin to hold, then sew along the 2 folded edges— sandwich in the pleated edge of the hemmed oblong in the middle of the strip as you sew (b).

9 Sew a narrow hem around the white fabric circle, then gently gather a circle of stitches 1 cm (½″) from edge (c).

10 Dress your hedgehog, tacking (basting) the cap in position to hold. Press in prickle pins to complete the pincushion.

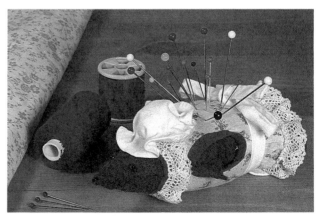

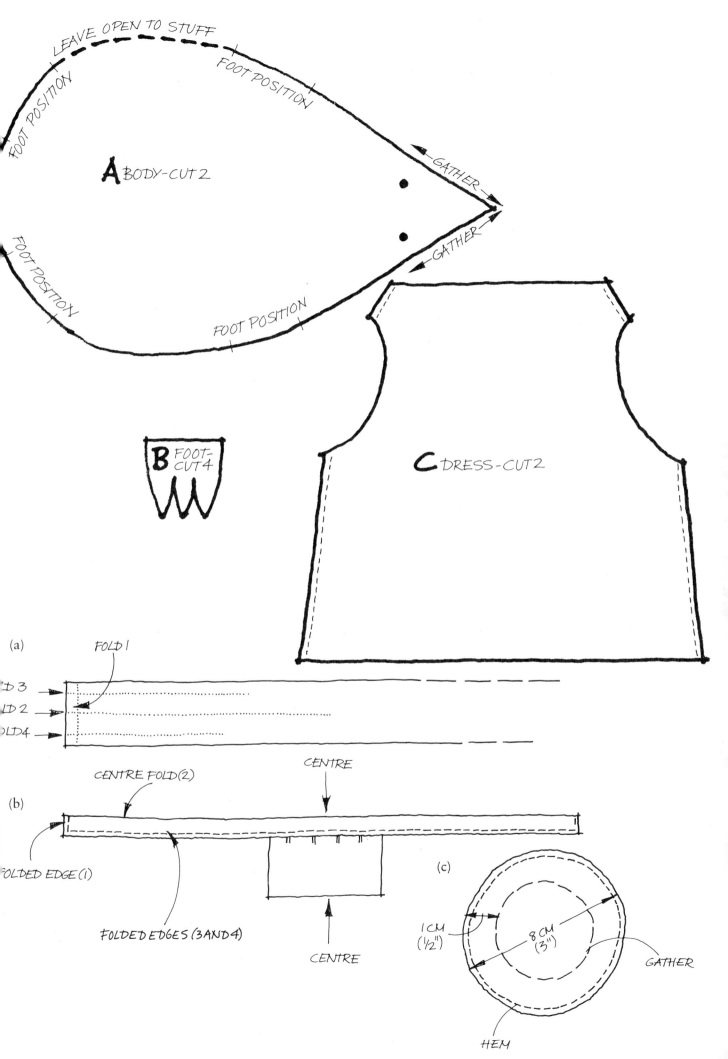

LEAVE OPEN TO STUFF

FOOT POSITION

FOOT POSITION

A BODY-CUT 2

GATHER

GATHER

FOOT POSITION

FOOT POSITION

FOOT POSITION

B FOOT-CUT 4

C DRESS-CUT 2

(a)

FOLD 1

'D 3

ID 2

OLD 4

CENTRE FOLD (2)

CENTRE

(b)

FOLDED EDGE (1)

FOLDED EDGES (3 AND 4)

CENTRE

(c)

1 CM (½")

8 CM (3")

GATHER

HEM

Pressed Flower Book Covers

White paper will show the subtle shades of petals best, but you might find that certain other colours contrast well.

3 Place the flowers on the front of the covered book, moving them around until you have the prettiest arrangement. Stick them down with a tiny blob of clear glue. (You only need enough to hold them in place while you arrange the flowers on the back and prepare the plastic [contact paper] covering.) Stick flowers on the back cover too.

4 Cover the book carefully with the clear plastic (contact paper), following the instructions on the roll. Be careful not to move or fold over any of the loose petals though. Trim so the plastic completely covers the first paper covering.

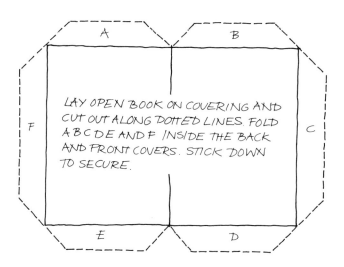

LAY OPEN BOOK ON COVERING AND CUT OUT ALONG DOTTED LINES. FOLD A B C D E AND F INSIDE THE BACK AND FRONT COVERS. STICK DOWN TO SECURE.

Timmy Willie was a little country mouse, born and bred in a beautiful garden. His one trip to town (in a vegetable hamper) was definitely a mistake, and he was only too pleased to get back to his peaceful home among the roses and pinks and pansies. You can use flowers to decorate the *outside* of a precious book. This could be a diary, album, notebook, message pad or school book. Either collect different leaves and flowers throughout the year or pick and press a bunch of the same kind.

To make pressed flower book covers you will need:
some freshly picked flowers, leaves or petals
absorbent paper, such as blotting paper
a pile of heavy books or a flower press
a book to cover
white or coloured paper
scissors and clear sticky tape
clear glue
clear self-adhesive plastic (contact paper)

1 Sandwich the flowers, leaves or petals individually between the sheets of absorbent paper in a flower press, or place carefully inside a heavy book and then put a pile of books on top. For maximum effect, try to open the flower heads up as you lay them out between the blotting paper sheets. Leave the flowers (untouched!) for several weeks to dry out completely. Treat them with great care when you finally remove them, as petals tend to be very fragile when dried.

2 Cover the book you have chosen with paper in the usual way as shown in the diagram above.

Padded Raffia Hangers

You'd think that naughty kittens who'd been sent to their room in disgrace would behave in a meek and mild manner, wouldn't you? Not so – Tom and his sisters Moppet and Mittens created havoc and made such a lot of noise doing so that they disturbed their mother's tea party which was going on below. Mrs. Tabitha Twitchit wouldn't let them get away with such behaviour though, and several hours must have been spent tidying away the clothes littered all over the floor.

To make a padded raffia hanger you will need:
a wire hanger
cotton wool (cotton batting)
clear glue
raffia
approx 2 m (2 yards) gold yarn (or similar)
ribbon

1 Cover the hanger with cotton wool (batting). A pleated strip torn in half lengthwise is the easiest to use. A few blobs of glue will hold the cotton wool roughly in place. Leave the hook part uncovered, though.

2 Stick one end of the raffia to the hanger with some glue. Wind the raffia tightly over the cotton wool and wire, easing the raffia open into a wide strip as you wind. Cover the entire hanger including the unpadded hook part at least twice. Secure the other raffia end with a touch of glue.

3 Wind contrasting gold (or other) yarn over the raffia. Start and end with a knot at the hook base.

4 Cover the knots with a ribbon bow.

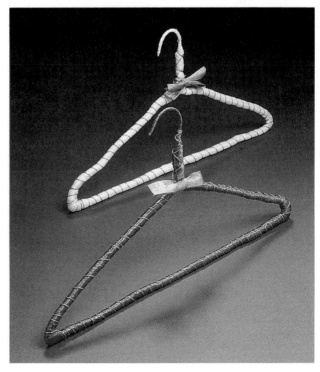

Jemima Puddle-duck Egg Cosy

All that poor, simple Jemima Puddle-duck wanted to do was hatch her own eggs, but her efforts to find a quiet place by herself led her into the clutches of a foxy gentleman with sandy whiskers. Although she escaped, and eventually managed to hatch 4 chicks herself, Jemima was never a very good sitter. A Jemima Puddle-duck egg cosy is, however, an excellent way of keeping a freshly-boiled egg deliciously warm.

To make a Jemima Puddle-duck egg cosy you will need:
tracing paper, pencil and scissors for paper
dressmaker's (chalk) pencil (if you have one)
white, pink, blue and yellow felt
2 small beads for eyes
feathers
pins and scissors for fabric
needle and thread
or fabric glue (if you don't want to sew the pieces on to your egg cosy)

1 Trace shapes A, B, C and D, cut them out and use the dressmaker's (chalk) pencil to draw round each tracing paper piece twice on the felt colours indicated. If you do not have a dressmaker's pencil, pin the pieces directly on to the felt and cut all 8 pieces out. You can sew *or* stick the pink, blue and yellow pieces on to the white cosy (A). Jemima must match on the front and back of the cosy so each half should look like the diagrams in (a) (see also the photograph on page 12).

2 *TO SEW* the pieces on to the cosy, place one each of the pink, yellow and blue pieces on one of the white cosy pieces and sew as indicated by . . . . on the first *three* diagrams shown, in (b) and (c). Do the same on the second white cosy piece, reversing the image as shown in (a). Then with right sides

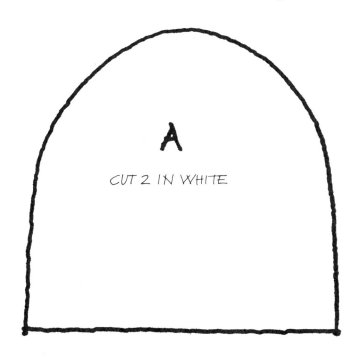

A

CUT 2 IN WHITE

10

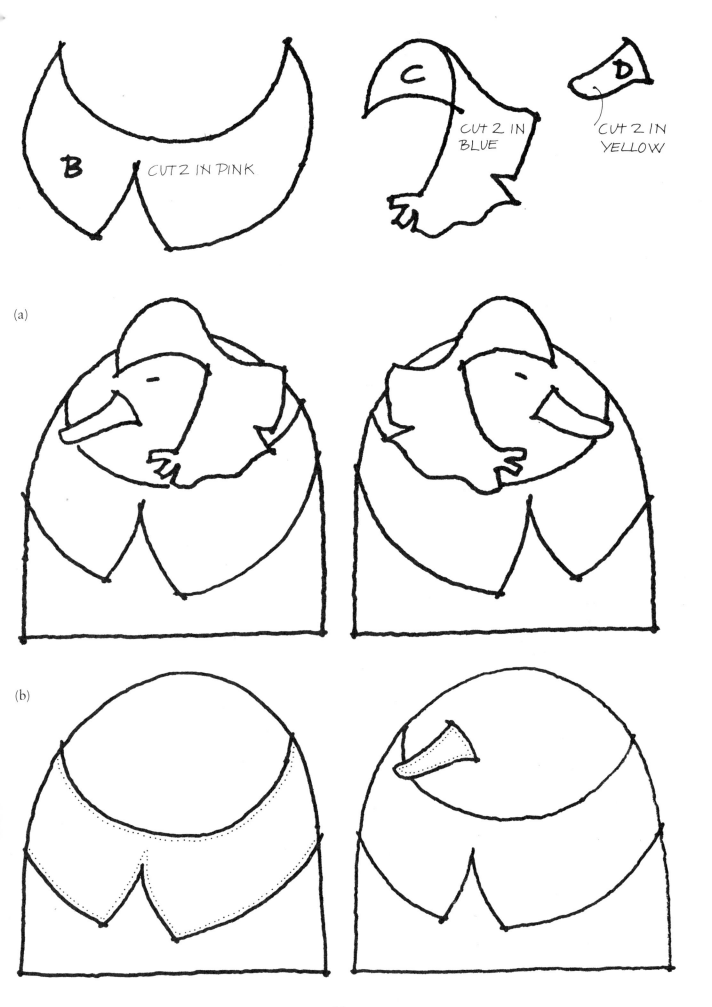

B CUT 2 IN PINK

C CUT 2 IN BLUE

D CUT 2 IN YELLOW

(a)

(b)

11

(c)

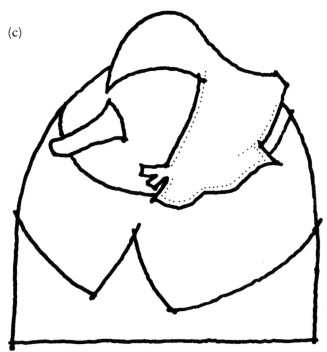
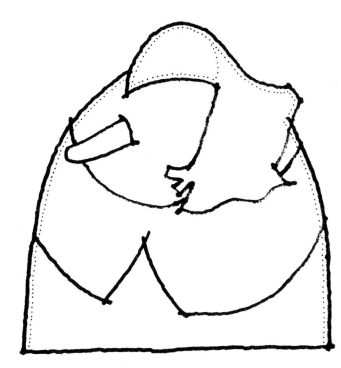

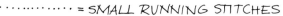 = SMALL RUNNING STITCHES

outwards, sew around the edge of the cosy, through all thicknesses, as indicated by . . . . on the last diagram in (c).

3 *TO STICK* the pieces on to the cosy, place the 2 white sections on top of each other and sew all around the curved edge. Stick the pink, yellow and blue pieces in position, remembering to reverse the image on the second side.

4 Sew the bead eyes on to each side of the cosy.

5 Snip the feathers into short lengths if they are large and sew or stick them by the spines around the bottom of the cosy, leaving the fluffy parts free.

Furry Mouse Mittens

The little Flopsy Bunnies could very easily have ended up as supper for the McGregors if clever Mrs. Tittlemouse hadn't nibbled an escape hole in the bottom corner of the sack that Mr. McGregor had put them in. For a thank-you present, the grateful parents, Flopsy and Benjamin Bunny, gave Thomasina Tittlemouse some rabbit wool. She used it to make herself a warm winter wardrobe: a cloak and hood, a handsome muff, and a pair of mittens.

To make a pair of furry mouse mittens you will need:
pencil, paper and scissors for paper
20 cm (8″) fur fabric (76 cm or 30″ wide)
pins, needle and scissors for fabric
embroidery thread
2 small beads for eyes ⎫
a little cotton wool ⎭ if you want to add mice

1 Place your hand on a piece of paper with your fingers spread slightly apart. Then, allowing about half an inch between your hand and the mitten outline, draw a mitten shape around your hand; be generous with the space surrounding your thumb. Make sure that the bottom of the mitten opening is as wide as the widest part of your hand, or you won't be able to get your hand in! Cut out the mitten pattern.

2 Pin the mitten pattern on to the fabric and cut the piece out. Cut a second piece out the same way. Then turn the pattern over and cut out 2 more pieces (a).

3 If you want to hide a mouse on one or both mittens, cut the mouse shape (b) in the right size to fit nicely on your glove and a long thin tail out of fur fabric. Pin on to one of the furry mitten pieces, and then sew on with blanket stitches (c), tucking

some cotton whiskers under the mouse snout and stuffing a small piece of cotton wool into its body as you sew around it. Catch one end of the tail in the stitching to secure it. Sew 2 bead eyes in position.

4 Place 2 matching mitten pieces on top of one another, furry sides out, and sew the pieces together around the curved edges and thumb using blanket stitch. Remember to leave the bottom open, but finish all round the open bottom edges in blanket stitch too.

(a)

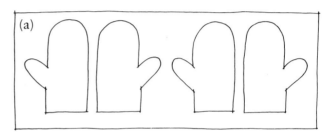

(b)

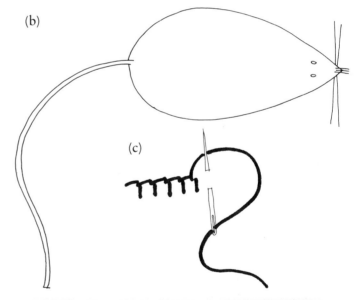

(c)

Button Card Presents

To make a button card present you will need:
thin white card
pencil, ruler, scissors for paper
coloured papers and glue, or felt pens
novelty buttons (or ordinary ones)
needle and thread

1 Cut a rectangle out of blank white card, but remember to check the size of envelopes first if you want to mail the card. 15 × 22 cm (6″ × 9″) folded in half is a convenient size.

2 Think of a scene to suit your buttons then draw or stick a torn or cut paper collage of it on the front of the card, including the buttons in your design. You could use animal or fun-shaped buttons – otherwise use round (or square) ones as wheels, faces, balls etc.

M rs. Tabitha Twitchit's 3 little kittens did not like being dressed up at all. In fact her very naughtiest son Tom found it particularly uncomfortable because he had grown rather too fat for his smart blue suit. His mother sewed on the buttons that had burst off before sending Tom and his sisters out to play. However, the kittens could not stay out of mischief for any time at all and Tom shed the newly-repaired buttons of his suit left and right.

3 Mark the button positions on the card with the point of a needle, then remove the buttons and push the needle through to make a hole. Make a large knot at the end of a double thread and sew the buttons on to the card. Knot tightly to secure them.

4 Don't forget to remind the person you are giving the card to, to *use* the buttons when they have finished enjoying your picture!

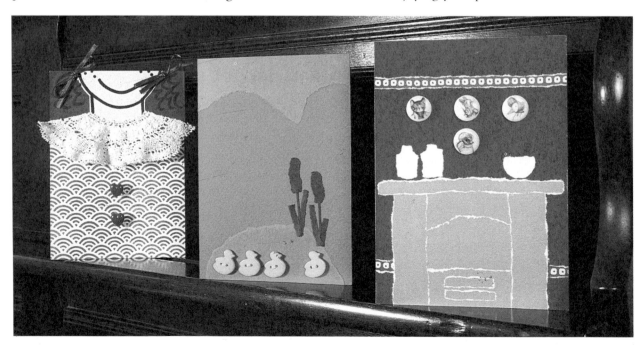

Timmy Tiptoes Leaf Mug and Tile

Timmy Tiptoes was a fat comfortable grey squirrel who lived with his wife Goody among the treetops in a very cosy nest, thatched with leaves. One autumn day, they were out gathering nuts for the coming winter, when Timmy was chased away by some other squirrels. Poor Goody was beside herself with worry, and searched high and low for him through the leafy trees and bushes.

To make a Timmy Tiptoes leaf mug and tile you will need:

apron or overall
a plain white mug and/or ceramic tile
small leaf
enamel paint
stick (or similar object) to stir paint
fine brush and a brush about 1 cm ($\frac{1}{2}$") wide
white spirit (turpentine)
rag and old jam jar (for cleaning brushes etc)
old newspapers
absorbent paper, such as tissue or paper towels
surgical gloves (available from large chemists) or *thin* rubber gloves
fabric glue and a piece of felt the same size as tile

1 Enamel paint is permanent when dry and therefore very difficult to remove from clothes, skin or work surfaces. So, protect yourself by wearing an apron or overall and thin rubber or surgical gloves. Cover all work surfaces with lots of newspaper too.

2 Read the instructions on the side of the can, then stir the paint well and brush the veined side of the leaf evenly with it. Blot the leaf on newspaper then position it, paint side down, on the mug. Lay the absorbent paper on top of the leaf and press firmly – try not to move the leaf, though, because the image will smudge. Remove the paper and leaf carefully and repeat the print process. Do not worry if your first prints are not perfect. You can wipe the images off with a rag dampened with white spirit (turpentine) while the paint is still wet. Use the fine brush to add or lengthen stalks, cleaning it in white spirit after use.

Although mugs are nice to drink out of they do tend to leave sticky rings on the table top. If you make a matching tile for your mug you could leave it beside your bed, on your desk, or wherever you often like a drink, and use it to put your mug on.

3 Print leaves on to the tile in the same way as the mug. You can fill in the background with a fine paint splatter if you like. This is done by dipping the end of the wide brush into the paint and gently flicking the bristles with your finger. Hold the brush about 3–5 cm (1"–2") above the tile to do this and make sure that you have *lots* of newspaper under and around it.

4 To finish off, stick a piece of felt on the back of the tile when the paint is dry (following the instructions on the glue pack). This will prevent it slipping and scratching any fragile surfaces.

Tailor of Gloucester Flower Tapestries

The poor old Tailor of Gloucester thought he'd lost his chance to make a fortune when he recovered from a fever on Christmas morning. He had been asked to make a coat and waistcoat for the mayor of Gloucester, who was to be married that day, and he had fallen ill before it was finished. But when the Tailor and his cat Simpkin went into the workshop, they found the most beautiful embroidered coat and waistcoat ever, ready and waiting. On them were roses and pansies, poppies and cornflowers, and buttonholes sewn in stitches so tiny and neat it looked as if mice had been at work!

To make a rose, poppy, pansy or cornflower tapestry you will need:

21 × 24 cm or 8″ × 10″ (approx) single thread tapestry
   canvas @ 10 squares per 25 mm (1″)
tapestry needle and scissors
graph paper   } if you want – see
pencil, paints and/or felt pens } below
thick tapestry yarn in the following colours:
Rose tapestry purple, navy, yellow, orange, olive green and bright green
Poppy tapestry navy, light and dark red, green, bright blue, purple and yellow
Pansy tapestry purple, red, yellow, black, green and violet
Cornflower tapestry turquoise, pink, light blue, purple, green and navy

Note: the large tapestry charts to be found on the endpapers of this book and on page 2 are for people who have already sewn some tapestries. Beginners are advised to start with the simpler designs pictured on these pages.

1 You may find the diagrams easier to follow if you copy them on to graph paper in the correct colours. The rows can then be crossed off as they are completed. If you have graph paper the same scale as the canvas (i.e. inches divided into tenths) you can transfer the picture on to it and then copy the correct colours and shapes on the canvas in felt pen. Otherwise, just start somewhere in the middle and follow the chart stitch by stitch.

2 All the tapestries are worked in a simple diagonal stitch called tent stitch. This runs from bottom left to top right of one square to another. The yarn should also run diagonally on the back, so work the rows from right to left following the number sequence in (a) on page 17. Turn the canvas upside down for the next row rather than reverse directions.

3 Don't pull the stitches too tight and if the yarn gets twisted, hold the canvas in mid-air horizontally, allowing the needle and yarn to hang down freely and untwist themselves.

4 When starting a new piece of yarn, do not make a knot in it, but leave a centimetre or so at the back and secure the yarn by sewing the first few stitches over it. To finish, thread the yarn through a few completed stitches at the back of the tapestry and cut off the rest.

5 Avoid jumping across the canvas from one area of colour to another. If the areas are not too far apart, weave through the stitches at the back. Alternatively, begin the new colour afresh.

6 Do not worry if the canvas becomes misshapen when sewn. This can be put right by stretching it (see below).

To stretch a tapestry canvas you will need:
piece of wood (blockboard or similar) cut to the

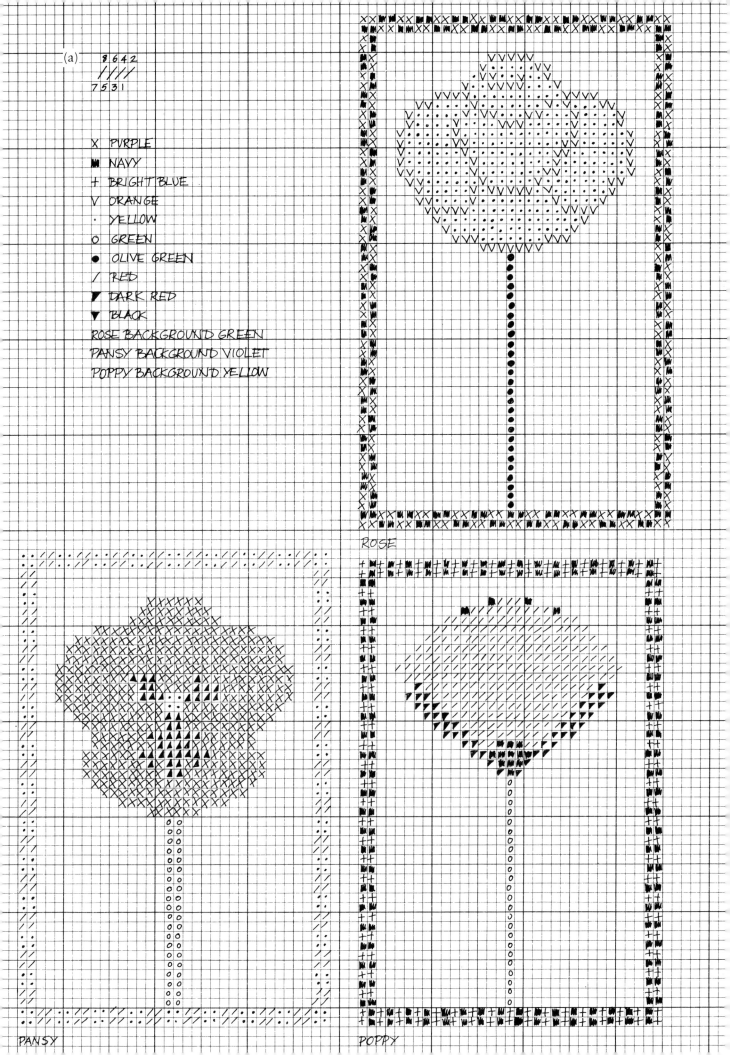

(a)

8 6 4 2
/ / / /
7 5 3 1

X PURPLE
M NAVY
+ BRIGHT BLUE
V ORANGE
· YELLOW
O GREEN
● OLIVE GREEN
/ RED
◢ DARK RED
▼ BLACK

ROSE BACKGROUND GREEN
PANSY BACKGROUND VIOLET
POPPY BACKGROUND YELLOW

ROSE

PANSY

POPPY

exact size that the finished tapestry should be, i.e. for the larger designs on the end papers, 16 × 18 cm (6³⁄₁₀″ × 7³⁄₁₀″)
small nails or tacks and hammer
fine water sprayer
hand-washing solution, such as Stergene

Ask an adult to help you with this project.

1 Mix about 1 teaspoonful of the washing solution with half a pint of water in the (clean) sprayer.

2 Line one edge of the sewn part of the tapestry up along a corresponding edge of the wood. Hammer nails or tacks along the unsewn part of this edge to hold the tapestry in position.

3 Dampen the tapestry with the sprayer, then pull it into shape over the wood and nail all round. Wet the tapestry well again with the washing solution and water spray then leave it for several days to dry out completely.

4 Remove the tacks and frame the tapestry (or use as you please!).

You can frame your single flowers as miniatures, or you could sew them on to clothes in cross stitch using embroidery thread (a fabric with holes in it such as Acrtex is ideal for this – see Introduction photograph).

18

Papier Mâché Tea Tray

The little country mouse Timmy Willie found life in a town-house much too frightening, with all the clatter and bustle, and the presence of a cat. Johnny Town-mouse and his friends tried to make him feel at home, but poor Timmy felt he could never be as daring and carefree as they were. They even came boldly out to enjoy an evening treat, collecting the sugar and smears of jam left on the carpet after Sarah the maid had tumbled down the stairs holding the tea tray.

To make a papier mâché tea tray you will need:
apron or overall
a tin tray
vaseline
old newspapers
wallpaper paste
water and receptacle to mix paste up in
scissors
enamel paint
stickers, doilies, coloured papers or white paper and
    felt pens
paper glue
clear gloss varnish
white spirit (turpentine) and brush

1 Papier mâché is messy to make, so wear an apron and cover the work surfaces with newspaper.

2 Smear a little vaseline all over the top of the tray. This will make the papier mâché easier to lift off when it is dry.

3 Make up some wallpaper paste according to the instructions on the packet.

4 Tear some old newspapers up into long, narrow strips 1–2 cm ($\frac{1}{2}''$–$1''$) wide, soak them in the paste then smooth on to the tray. Build up lots of layers – you will need to use several whole newspapers to make the tray strong enough. Try to lay the strips evenly, positioning one layer across the tray then the next layer in the opposite direction. Work right up to the edge and do not worry about overlapping it. If you find that you have not applied enough layers in one go you can add more at a later stage.

5 When you are sure that the tray will be thick enough (at least $\frac{1}{2}$ cm or $\frac{1}{4}''$), leave it to dry and harden completely. This will take several days.

6 Carefully lever the papier mâché tray from the tin one. Wash the vaseline off the tin tray.

7 Trim the edge off the papier mâché tray carefully with a sharp knife or scissors and paint it with enamel paint. Do the bottom first, let it dry then turn over and paint the top surface. Let it dry again.

8 Apply a design or picture on the tray using stickers, pieces of doily or by cutting or tearing coloured shapes to stick on the surface. Alternatively, use felt pens to colour designs on white paper then tear or cut out and stick down in the same way.

9 Cover the entire surface of the tray with a coat of clear gloss varnish to protect it. Try this out in a corner first as it may discolour your paper a bit.

Mrs. Tittlemouse Mobile

Busy Mrs. Thomasina Tittlemouse (who was terribly tidy and particular) lived in a bank under a hedge where she spent most of her time clearing and tidying, sweeping and scrubbing and dusting. Her life was made much more difficult by all the uninvited guests she had to shoo away. As well as visits from spiders and beetles with dirty feet, Miss Butterfly liked to settle on her sugar bowl, Mother Ladybird ran up and down outside, and bees buzzed around her empty storeroom – especially the extremely buzzy Babbitty Bumble who sent her into a complete tizzy.

To make a Mrs. Tittlemouse mobile you will need:
compass
blue, black, yellow, red and white thin card (or stiff
   paper)
black felt pen, pencil, ruler, scissors for paper
clear all purpose glue
small cardboard inner roll
needle and white thread
14 black sequins
black string or yarn

The 'sky hat'

1 Set the compass to 9 cm (4″) and draw a circle on the blue card. Mark a line from the centre point to the edge. Cut the circle out and cut down the marked line (which should be 9 cm or 4″ long!).

2 Draw about 9 puffy cloud shapes on white card. Cut them out and stick them, half on and half off, round the edge of the blue circle. Start and end at the cut line.

3 Overlap the 2 cut edges of the blue circle about 3 cm or 1½″ (to form a shallow cone shape) and glue to hold. Bend the overlapped part of the clouds down over the edge of the circle.

The bees

4 Set the compass to 3 cm (1½″) then draw and cut out 3 yellow circles. Fold each one in half. Cut or tear 6 black strips about 1 × 6 cm (½″ × 3″) and glue them over the fold across the centre of the yellow circles (2 for each bee).

5 Cut or tear 6 small white circles (a little larger than the sequins) for eyes and glue one on either side of the fold at one end of each bee circle. Stick a sequin on top of each white circle.

6 Cut 3 × 6 cm (1½″ × 3″) lengths of the black yarn, fold each piece in half and stick between the fold, below the eyes on each bee. Trim the antennae to even lengths if necessary.

7 Cut out or tear 6 small white wings (in a pear shape about 2 cm or 1″ long) and stick the narrow ends on to the front black bee stripe (one on each side) so that the wider part of the wing can flap freely above the fold.

The ladybirds

8 Set the compass to 3 cm (1½″) again and cut out 3 red circles. Fold each one in half then glue 3 cut or torn black paper or card spots on each side. Add eyes and antennae as for the bees (see numbers 5 and 6 above).

The butterfly and sugar bowl

9 Set the compass to 5 cm (2″), draw and cut out a circle from blue card. Cut a quarter of it out (a) and stick the two straight edges together to form the sugar bowl. It's easiest to work with this cone-shaped bowl if you balance it on the end of a cardboard roll (b) while you make and assemble its contents.

10 Make some sugar cubes by copying shape (c) on to white card. Mark the dotted lines with a pencil spot at the edges. Cut out, then put some glue on sections A, C and E. Fold at the dotted lines and stick A to B, C to D and E to F.

11 Trace and cut out a butterfly shape from black card (d) then fold it in half along the dotted line. Stick on some red wing markings, then eyes and antennae like the bees and ladybirds. To assemble the sugar bowl contents, crumple a piece of white paper up and place it in the bottom of the bowl. Stick on some paper sugar cubes and glue the butterfly on top.

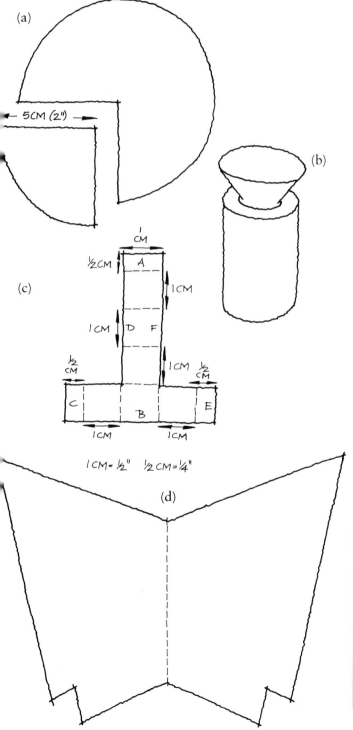

(a)

← 5CM (2") →

(b)

(c)

CM
½CM   A
1CM
1CM   D   F
½CM   1CM   ½CM
C   B   E
1CM   1CM

1CM = ½"   ½ CM = ¼"

(d)

12 Finish the mobile by first threading a double piece of thread with a large knot in it through a point at the top edge of the sugar bowl. Take the thread through the centre of the blue 'sky hat' (upwards from underneath and then downwards to make a small stitch) and down again to the other side of the sugar bowl. Check that the bowl is hanging straight then tie a knot to secure it. Do the same thing on the opposite side of the bowl to balance it.

13 Pass a double piece of thread with a large knot in it through the central compass point of each bee and ladybird. Start under each circle between the fold and thread up through a point in the bend of a cloud. Make a small stitch downwards and knot under the cloud.

14 Space the bees and ladybirds alternately, equal distances apart, around the cloud circle. Hang the insects opposite each other on thread that is the same length so that the mobile balances.

15 Finally, sew a loop of cotton upwards from under the centre of the 'sky hat' and knot it so that you can hang your mobile up.

Mrs. Rabbit's Lavender Bag

Flopsy, Mopsy, Cotton-tail and Peter Rabbit's mother, Mrs. Rabbit, was a widow. She earned her living by making and selling country goods. These included various herbs, rosemary tea and rabbit-tobacco (which is what *we* call lavender). Indeed, she may well have used the herbs or lavender to make sweet smelling bags for keeping between the piles of fresh laundry in her drawers or cupboards.

To make a patchwork lavender bag you will need:
thin card and paper
compass, pencil, ruler and scissors for paper
needle, cotton, pins and scissors for fabric
lavender coloured fabric scraps in 4 designs
dried lavender
19 lavender sequins
lavender ribbon ⎫
a lace butterfly ⎭ optional

1 Any combination of shapes can be used for a patchwork, provided they 'lock' together (like tiles on a floor). Squares are the simplest shape to use, but hexagons form a pretty flower pattern. For the hexagon on this patchwork, set the compass to 1 cm ($\frac{1}{2}$"). Draw a circle on the card, then with the compass at the same setting, place the point somewhere on the circle and mark the spot where the

compass pencil touches the circle further on. Move the compass point to this spot and mark the circle again. Continue around the circle till you have 6 marks then rule lines between the spots to form a hexagon as (a).

2 Cut the card hexagon out and draw round it on the card 38 times. Cut each of the 38 identical hexagons out too.

3 Make a *paper* hexagon (by drawing round the first hexagon again on paper and cutting out) and use this as a pattern for cutting the fabric out. Pin the paper hexagon on to the fabric and cut a hexagon shape, adding a border of about $\frac{1}{2}$ cm ($\frac{1}{4}$") along each side, as shown by the broken line in (b). You will need 14 hexagons in the first fabric, 12 hexagons in the second fabric and 6 hexagons in the third and fourth fabrics.

4 Tack (baste) each fabric hexagon on to a cardboard one, turning in the $\frac{1}{2}$ cm ($\frac{1}{4}$") border to hold it in place (c).

5 With right sides facing, oversew 2 hexagons together in small stitches along one edge only (d). Open the 2 hexagons out and place a third in position. Flip it (right sides together) over the first hexagon and oversew the joining edge (e). Oversew adjoining edges of the second and third hexagons in the same way (f) then keep adding hexagons to form the flower pattern shown in (g). Sew the remaining hexagons together in the same way for the other side of the lavender bag.

6 Place the 2 hexagon flowers right sides together and oversew around the edge leaving an opening for the filling. Undo the tacking (basting) and remove the cardboard hexagon shapes.

7 Strip the lavender heads off their stalks and use them to fill the patchwork bag. Sew up the opening.

8 Sew a sequin on the centre of each hexagon and decorate one side of the bag with bows and/or lace if you like.

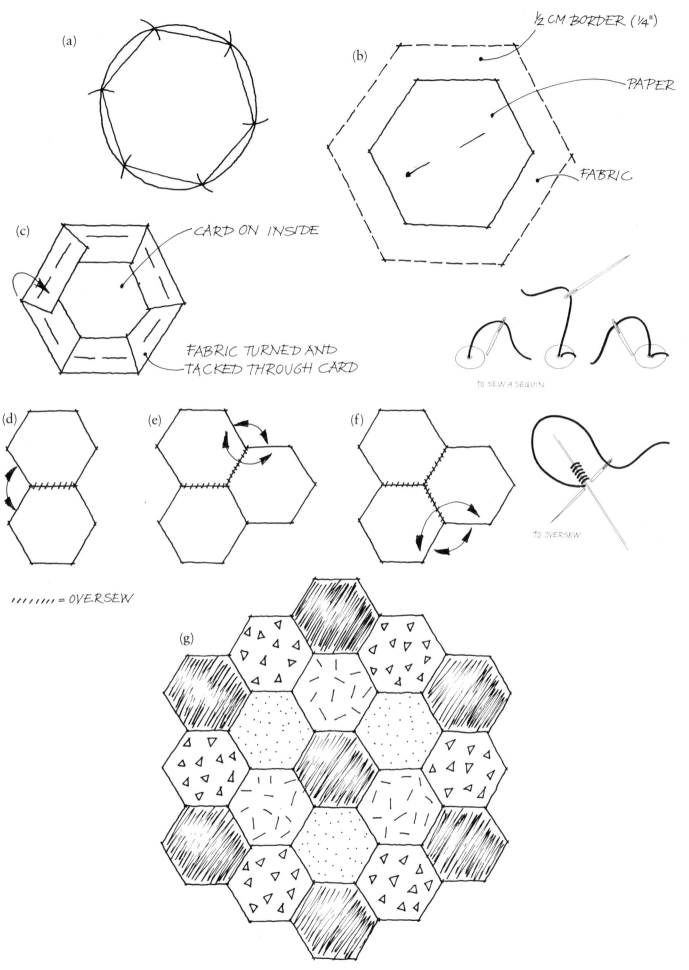

(a)

(b) ½ CM BORDER (¼")

PAPER

FABRIC

(c) CARD ON INSIDE

FABRIC TURNED AND
TACKED THROUGH CARD

TO SEW A SEQUIN

(d)   (e)   (f)

TO OVERSEW

∕∕∕∕∕∕∕ = OVERSEW

(g)

Mrs. Rabbit's Lavender bag

Bunch of Flowers Brooch

When Ribby the Pussy-cat asked the little black dog Duchess to come to tea, Duchess decided to take some flowers as a present. The flower beds in her beautiful front garden were packed with summer blooms, and she picked a lovely bunch to take with her.

To make a bunch of flowers brooch you will need:
a ring (curtain ring, keyring or similar)
embroidery threads (including green)
needle and scissors
small gold safety pin

1 First cover the ring with close buttonhole stiches: tie the embroidery thread to the ring to begin, then hold the ring vertically and bring the needle through the centre from back to front (a). Twist the thread (from the eye of the needle) round the needle (b) and pull tight. Continue the stitches round the ring and secure with a knot.

2 Sew 4 or 5 strands of green thread close together across the centre of the ring, catching the buttonhole stitches at the bottom and top to hold (c).

3 Continue with the green horizontally across the vertical strands to fill in the top quarter of the ring (d). Catch the buttonhole stitches at either side in the same manner as (c).

4 In various contrasting colours, cover the right side of the top green quarter with french knots: starting on the right side, make a tiny stitch down and up through the work, but before pulling the needle and thread through, wind the thread (fairly tightly) around it 3 or 4 times (e). Pull the needle through the loops to make a firm raised knot. Complete the stitch by inserting the needle again, as close to the knot as possible, then come up again to make the next knot, or knot underneath the work and start again with a new colour.

5 Tie a thread around the centre of the 'stalks' to finish the 'bunch of flowers'.

6 Sew along one side of the safety pin to hold it on the back of the 'flower heads'. Use this to attach the brooch to your clothes, bags, belts, hats etc.

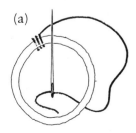
(a)

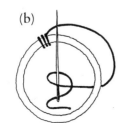
(b)

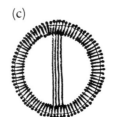
(c)

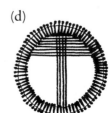
(d)

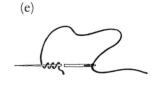
(e)

25

Tie-Dye Socks

Mrs. Tiggy-winkle was an excellent laundry-woman and had lots of customers who supplied her with a never-ending stream of clothes to wash. On the day that little Lucie visited her, Mrs. Tiggy-winkle had a pile of clothes to launder: among them, Cock Robin's scarlet waistcoat, Tabby Kitten's mittens, Peter Rabbit's blue jacket, and last but not least, Sally Henny-penny's yellow stockings. Sally Henny-penny had been scratching around in the yard so much that the heels were nearly worn through, and Mrs. Tiggy-winkle thought she would soon be walking barefoot!

To tie-dye socks you will need:
apron, rubber gloves, old newspaper etc.
pair of white cotton or cotton mix socks (see 1 below)
fabric dye suitable for hand or cold water dyeing
4 tbls salt
water
bucket (or similar)
stick (or similar)
string, cotton, dried beans etc.
scissors

1 Cotton is the best fabric to dye although cotton mixtures produce a good result that is a few shades lighter. A white base will give the purest colours, but light coloured socks could be tie-dyed just as well.

2 A pack or tin of Dylon dye is enough for about 8 oz/250 g dry fabric. Check the weight of your socks – you should be able to dye about 3 pairs per colour. Try mixing and matching designs and colour combinations. If you use more than one colour, it is better to use ones which mix well such as red and yellow (to make orange), blue and yellow (to make green) etc. Otherwise you might end up with a rather muddy mess. Don't be frightened to experiment, though – surprising combinations can work well.

3 Wash and rinse the socks *even if they are new* because they will have been coated with a finish that prevents the dye being fully absorbed. For the actual dyeing process, follow the manufacturer's instructions on the packs, but do protect clothes, work surfaces and hands (wear gloves!) because the dye is extremely difficult to remove.

4 Prepare the socks while they are still damp. The basic idea is to stop dye reaching some parts of the fabric; and you can tie or bind the fabric in any way to produce all sorts of different patterns.
Sock (a) Scrunch into a tight ball and bind tightly with string. Dye in pink. Dry and untie then scrunch up again (differently to the first time) and bind. Dye in blue, dry and untie. Finally scrunch, bind and dye in jade green.
Sock (b) Put dried chickpeas inside the sock and tie round each one individually with string. Dye in jade green.
Sock (c) Fold lengthways like a concertina and tie at intervals with string. Dye in pink, dry and untie. Tie knots in the sock itself, close together down the entire length. Dye in yellow.
Sock (d) Dip the bottom three-quarters of untied sock into yellow dye, then hang on a line over a bucket or whatever the dye was mixed up in to catch drips. Leave to dry then dip the bottom half of sock into orange dye and leave to drip again. Finally, dip the bottom quarter into red dye and allow to drip and dry completely.

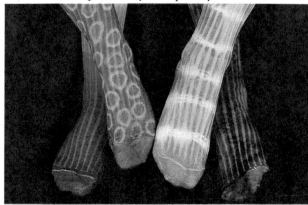

Sequinned Fish T-Shirt

1 Use the dressmaker's (chalk) pencil to draw a fish shape on the front (or back) of your T-shirt. You can either copy the shape from the illustration opposite, or enlarge the diagram (below left) by copying it on to graph paper with $\frac{1}{2}''$ squares. Then cut it out and draw round it on your T-shirt.

2 Fill the tail and fin areas in by sewing on gold beads, then sew some along the mouth line and also at intervals around the fish body.

3 Sew on the black sequin or button eye and the rest of the fish scales using the multicoloured sequins.

4 Sew a few extra silver sequins on to the T-shirt outside the fish part to catch the light if you like.

If Mr. Jeremy Fisher hadn't been wearing a mackintosh during his fishing expedition at the pond, a really *frightful* thing might have happened. For while Mr. Jeremy tried to catch some minnows for his dinner, an enormous trout nearly swallowed him whole. Luckily, this trout didn't like the taste of mackintoshes and only ate poor Mr. Jeremy's shiny goloshes!

To make a sequinned fish T-shirt you will need:
dressmaker's (chalk) pencil
a plain coloured T-shirt
needle, thread and scissors
multicoloured sequins
a large black sequin or button
straight gold beads

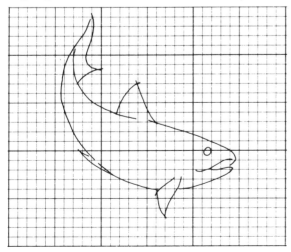

Onion-Stringing

Naughty Benjamin Bunny encouraged his cousin Peter Rabbit to go back into Mr. McGregor's garden to fetch his clothes, which Peter had lost there on a previous expedition. And while they were there, Benjamin even suggested they should take some onions home in Peter's red-spotted handkerchief as a present for his mother! Peter was too nervous to tie the bundle up properly and many of the onions fell out. Eventually, though, the rabbits got safely out of the garden and Mrs. Rabbit was so pleased to see her son arrive home safely that she forgave his disobedience, and strung up the onions that were left to hang from her ceiling with the bunches of herbs and rabbit tobacco.

To string onions you will need:
onions with green tops (see below)
about 2 m (2 yards) strong twine
scissors

1 Onions for stringing must still have their green tops (i.e. the part that grows above the earth) attached. These will wither to a brown straw-like strand when the onions are harvested. As the onions ripen, lift the bulbs, but leave them laid out on the earth for a week or so to dry out a little. If you do not grow your own onions ask a farmer or market gardener if you may buy some of his onions *before*

the tops are removed. Onions are usually harvested around September – alert him well in advance of your special request. You will need between 10 and 20 onions to make a nice string.

2 Fold the twine in half and lay it on a table. Tie the first onion into the loop at the bottom of the string as follows (see diagram below). Hold the onion in position behind the 2 halves of twine and pull the onion top through to the front (between the twine). Tightly fold the top to the right, around the back (both parts of twine), to the front again (from the left hand side). Then push it firmly through the centre front towards the back to secure it. Keep both halves of the twine together all along the string.

3 Twist the rest of the onions closely together along the string in the same way.

4 Trim some of the ragged ends off the onion tops, but leave a good few centimetres intact to hold the onions in place. Tie one knot in the twine at the top of the onions and another a bit further on so that the string can be hung up.

Fluffy Autumn Scarf

Squirrel Nutkin lost his tail one fine autumn day on Owl Island. He had travelled there over the lake with his brother Twinkleberry and numerous cousins because the leaves on the trees had been transformed into a glorious golden haze and the nuts were ripe for harvesting. The stripes on this scarf should be as richly coloured as falling leaves.

To knit a fluffy autumn scarf you will need:

approx 100 g (4 oz) mohair yarn in autumn shades
   (such as 25 g or 1 oz each of light brown, dark
   brown, orange and rust)
gold yarn
pair 5 mm knitting needles
darning needle
gold leaf-shaped sequins   ⎫
needle and cotton for sequins ⎭ if you like

1 Although the finished measurement of this scarf is flexible, you might want to knit a small tension square to check that your shape will be roughly right. So, cast on 9 stitches of mohair wool and knit 14 rows of plain knitting. This should make a 5 cm (2″) square. If your square is much larger, try using a smaller-sized pair of needles, or use larger needles if your square is much smaller.

2 This scarf is all knitted in plain. Cast on 30 stitches of mohair and knit for 5 cm or 2″ (i.e. 14 rows approx). Leave a few centimetres of mohair free to tie in the next colour and cut off the rest of the ball.

3 Knit 2 rows of gold, tying the 2 yarns together to begin. Knit another 5 cm (2″) in the second mohair colour followed by 2 rows of gold. Continue the stripes in this manner until you have used each colour, then repeat them in the same order.

4 The finished scarf should have about 24 mohair stripes and be approximately 130 cm (51″) long. Cast off the last row loosely. Use a darning needle to sew all the cut off ends in neatly, and sew the gold leaf-shaped sequins on here and there if you like.

5 To finish off add some fringes: Cut about 20, 10 cm (4″) lengths of mohair yarn in the colours of the last stripe at each end of the scarf. Attach the lengths one at a time by folding a piece of mohair wool in half. Push the folded part through one of the scarf's cast off (or on) stitches to make a loop (a), then tuck the 2 loose ends through the loop (b) and pull tight. Continue knotting lengths of mohair wool evenly along each short end of the scarf then trim the fringes to the same length.

(a)   (b)

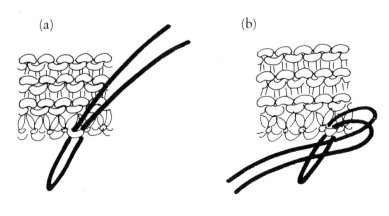

Family Tree Sampler

Peter Rabbit had lots and lots of relations. We do not know the names of some of them, such as his grandparents or great-grandparents, cousins, or great-aunts and great-uncles. However, we do know that his sisters were called Flopsy, Mopsy and Cotton-tail and his mother was called Mrs. Josephine Rabbit. We also know that his sister Flopsy married their cousin Benjamin (whose father Old Mr. Benjamin Bunny was Mrs. Rabbit's brother) and that *their* children were the Flopsy Bunnies.

It's far easier to explain these relationships in a family tree, with connecting lines to show who married whom, and who their children and grandchildren were. If you want to make a cross-stitch sampler, restrict yourself to your closest relatives, like parents, grandparents, brothers or sisters. Uncles, aunts and cousins might also be included, depending how many there are!

To make a family tree sampler you will need:
squared paper, pencil and felt pens or crayons
scissors for paper and clear sticky tape
cross stitch fabric
embroidery threads, needle and scissors
dressmaker's (chalk) pencil

1 First you must design your personal sampler. List the names you wish to include, then following the charted letters (a) draw each name out separately on squared paper. You can draw them in colour if this will help you plan the chart. Cut each name out carefully.

2 Lay the names in position to form your family tree on a clean sheet of squared paper (you may need 2 or more sheets stuck together) lining all the squares up accurately. Move the names about until you are happy with the basic layout then stick them down. Draw on the lines (in crosses) that indicate the family relationships together with other decorations such as a tree, circles, squares, or flowers (b). You may like to draw these out on another sheet and stick them on like the names. The family surname could go at the top of the sampler.

3 Samplers are usually vertical when finished (unlike Peter's, shown on page 32, which is horizontal). They also often have the sewer's initials and the date the sampler was completed. A decorative border helps to complete the picture.

4 To work out how much fabric you will need for the sampler, count the squares on each edge of the drawn picture and buy fabric with double the number of holes (each cross stitch needs 2) allowing a few extra all round. Decide which colours you are going to use if you have not already done so.

5 Copy the design on to the cross stitch fabric with the dressmaker's (chalk) pencil (or just work straight from the design, plotting the stitches as you go) then sew in cross stitch. This is a simple stitch, but should always be sewn in the same manner for an even finish, i.e. the second half of the stitch should cross the first half in the same direction. It's easiest to work the first half of all the stitches in one colour then cross them as a second stage (c).

6 Use all the strands of the embroidery thread or divide it in half or less depending on the weight of the fabric. However, don't be tempted to use very long pieces as it can tangle easily. Hold your work horizontally in mid-air with the needle and thread hanging down freely to untwist if necessary (like tapestry). Avoid pulling the stitches too tight.

7 When the sampler is complete, ask an adult to help you iron it on the wrong side under a damp cloth.

8 To prepare your work for framing, get a piece of hardboard cut to the finished size of the sampler. Lay the sampler on the board and fold the unsewn part round the edge to the back. Stitch the unsewn edge from top to bottom and side to side (or stick it) so that the sampler is held firmly in position.

NB. If you do not wish to sew a sampler you could still make a very effective family tree picture by just drawing the coloured crosses neatly on a large sheet of paper.